# A DORLING KINDERSLEY BOOK
Conceived, edited, and designed by DK Direct Limited

## Note to parents

**What's Inside? Insects** is designed to help young children
understand the fascinating secrets of insects' bodies.
It illustrates what is inside a caterpillar, how a
spiny stick insect lays eggs, and why a fly is able to walk
on the ceiling. It is a book for you and your child
to read and talk about together, and to enjoy.

**Designers**  Sonia Whillock and Juliette Norsworthy
**Typographic Designer**  Nigel Coath
**US Editor**  B. Alison Weir
**Editor**  Sarah Phillips
**Design Director**  Ed Day
**Editorial Director**  Jonathan Reed

**Illustrator**  Richard Manning
**Photographer**  Frank Greenaway
**Writer**  Angela Royston

Insects supplied by the Natural History Museum, London,
and Trevor Smith's Animal World

First American Edition, 1992

10 9 8 7 6 5 4 3 2 1

Dorling Kindersley, Inc., 232 Madison Avenue
New York, New York 10016

**Library of Congress Cataloging-in-Publication Data**
Insects. – 1st American ed.
    p.  cm. – (What's inside?)
Summary: Describes the behavior, anatomy, and inner workings of various
insects, including the honeybee, butterfly, and stick insect.
ISBN 1-56458-003-2
1. Insects – Juvenile literature.  2. Insects – Anatomy – Juvenile literature.
[1. Insects.]  I. Dorling Kindersley, Inc.  II. Series.
QL467.2.I58  1992
595.7 — dc20
                                                                91–58215
                                                                CIP
Printed in Italy                                                AC

# WHAT'S INSIDE?

# INSECTS

DORLING KINDERSLEY, INC.
NEW YORK

# BEETLE

This is a snout beetle. It is called this because of its big, funny "nose." Its jaws are at the end and it uses them to eat plants.

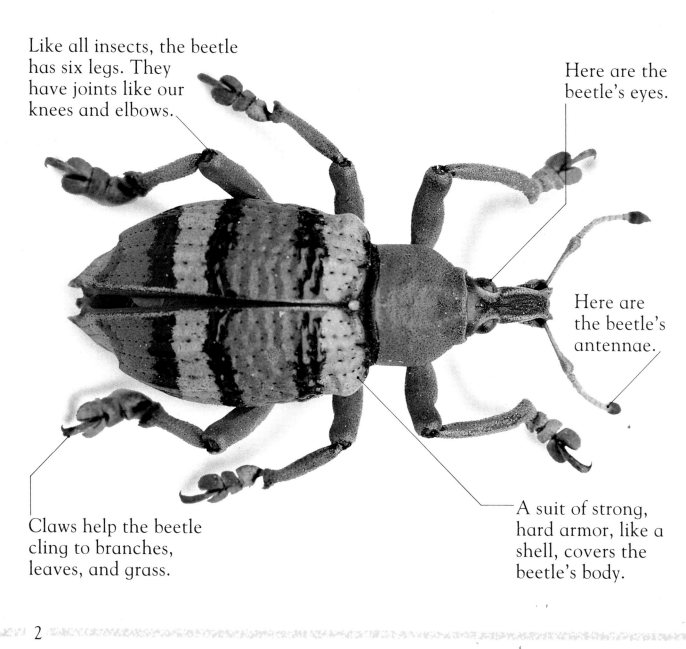

Like all insects, the beetle has six legs. They have joints like our knees and elbows.

Here are the beetle's eyes.

Here are the beetle's antennae.

Claws help the beetle cling to branches, leaves, and grass.

A suit of strong, hard armor, like a shell, covers the beetle's body.

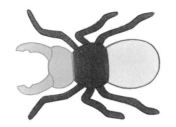

A beetle is an insect. Like all insects, its body has three parts: a head, a middle part, called the thorax, and a back end, called the abdomen.

Inside the beetle's hard shell, its body is soft. All parts of the body need blood, to bring food and take away waste.

This is the beetle's brain.

A beetle's heart is a long tube. From it, blood goes to all parts of the body.

# HONEYBEE

This honeybee lives in a hive with many other bees. It feeds on pollen and nectar which it collects from flowers. Both pollen and nectar are stored inside the hive, where the nectar is made into honey.

Black and yellow stripes warn birds and other animals that bees have a poisonous sting.

The bee sucks up sweet nectar with its long tongue.

The honeybee's body is covered with hair. Pollen sticks to the hairs as the bee pushes into the center of the flower.

Inside the hive are lots of rooms, where the honey and pollen are stored.

Poison for the bee's stinger is made here. It is the poison that makes the sting hurt.

This is the bee's honey stomach. It stores the nectar here until it takes it back to the hive.

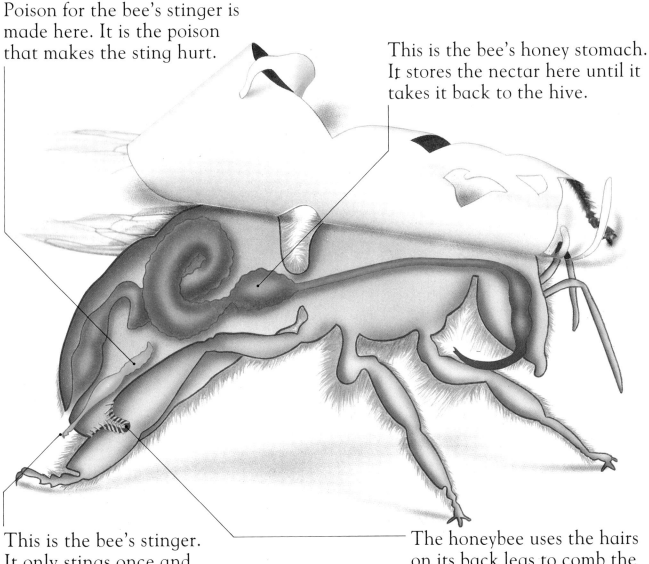

This is the bee's stinger. It only stings once and dies soon after.

The honeybee uses the hairs on its back legs to comb the pollen into this bag.

# CATERPILLAR

Like all insects, this caterpillar hatched out of an egg. Now it lives on leaves and spends most of its time eating. It is growing fast. Soon it will begin to change into a butterfly.

The caterpillar breathes through these holes along its sides. They are called spiracles. ———

As it grows, a caterpillar gets too big for its skin. First a new, larger skin grows underneath, then the old skin splits and the caterpillar crawls out and leaves it behind.

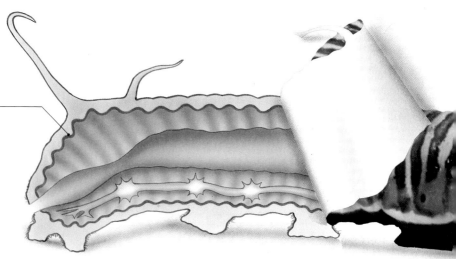

Birds leave this caterpillar alone. Its bright colors and tentacles trick them into thinking it's poisonous.

The caterpillar holds food with its front three pairs of legs. The other legs are for walking and holding on to leaves.

This is the caterpillar's food tube. It is very big because the caterpillar eats so much.

Nerves from here spread all over its body, so that the caterpillar can feel things around it.

# FLY

Have you ever wanted to walk on the ceiling like a fly? You would have to have a fly's sticky feet to do so. Many people kill flies because they spread germs.

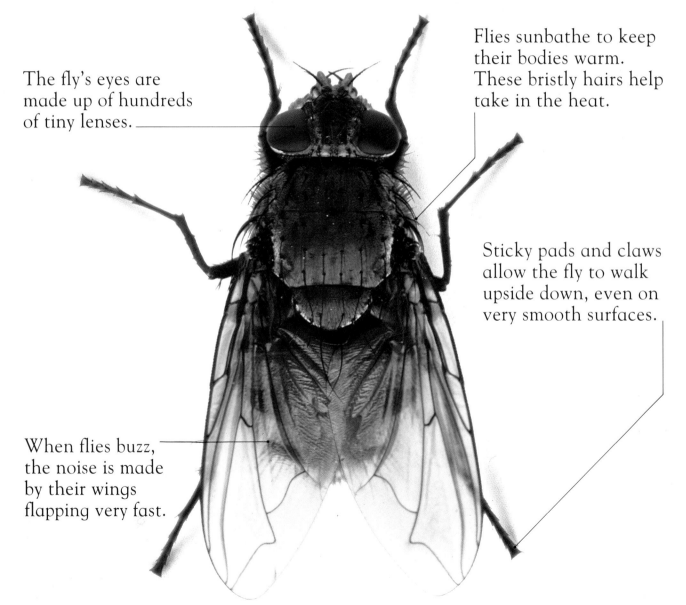

Flies sunbathe to keep their bodies warm. These bristly hairs help take in the heat.

The fly's eyes are made up of hundreds of tiny lenses.

Sticky pads and claws allow the fly to walk upside down, even on very smooth surfaces.

When flies buzz, the noise is made by their wings flapping very fast.

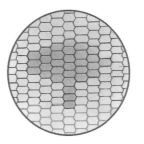

When a fly looks at something, it sees it broken up into lots and lots of little pieces, like a mosaic.

The fly breathes in and out through holes in its sides, called spiracles.

These are the fly's air sacs. They carry air to all parts of the body.

This fly, like some other insects, can taste with its feet.

9

# CRICKET

This bush cricket lives in rough, grassy places.
It comes out in the evening and eats plants.
If it senses danger, it will quickly hop away.

This cricket is green,
just like grass, which helps
it hide from birds that
would like to eat it.

Long antennae tell
the cricket what the
things around it
feel and smell like.

Crickets use
their long back
legs to leap away
from danger.

Crickets have
"ears" on their
front legs.

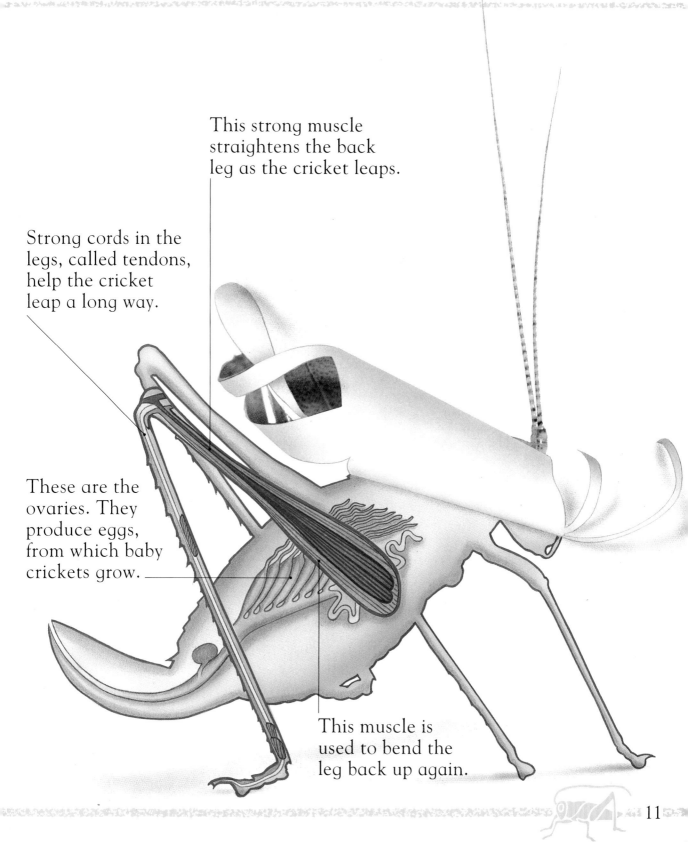

This strong muscle straightens the back leg as the cricket leaps.

Strong cords in the legs, called tendons, help the cricket leap a long way.

These are the ovaries. They produce eggs, from which baby crickets grow.

This muscle is used to bend the leg back up again.

11

# LADYBUG

Ladybugs are a kind of beetle. They live in forests, fields, parks, and gardens. Gardeners like ladybugs because they eat the aphids (small insects) that feed on garden plants.

Not all ladybugs have spots like this one. Some have stripes!

Ladybugs are brightly colored to warn birds and other animals that they taste bad.

The ladybug's hard back is really a pair of wings. They make a strong shield to keep the ladybug safe.

When a ladybug wants to fly, its hard front wings swing out to the sides. The hard wings do not flap, but they help lift the ladybug into the air.

Underneath the ladybug's hard back there are lots of nerves. They help the ladybug feel the things around it.

This is the ladybug's brain.

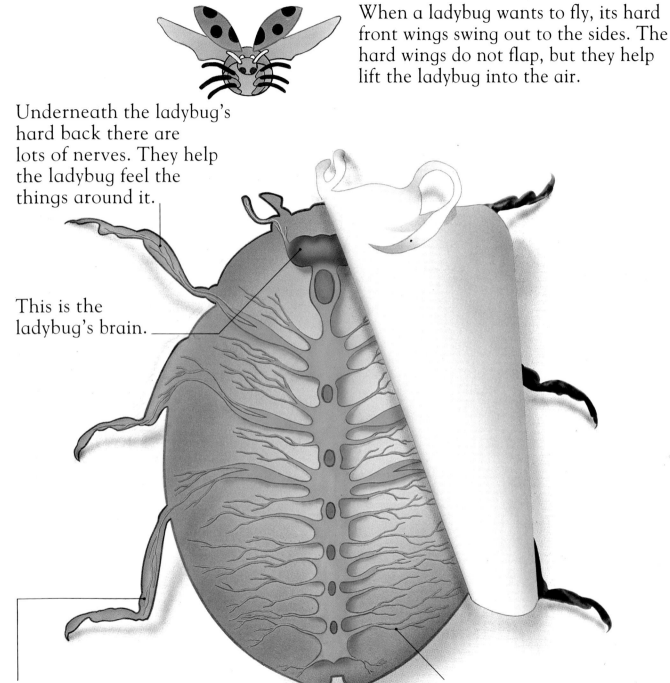

Nerves go all the way down the ladybug's legs. Others go to the tips of its antennae.

These nerves are like telephone wires. They carry messages around the body.

Hybrid tea rose
*Rosa* 'Splendid Renate'

Prairie gentian
*Eustoma, Lisianthus*

Transvaal daisy
*Gerbera* 'Stranger'

Conebush
*Leucadendron linifolium*

Persian buttercup
*Ranunculus*

Seeded *Eucalyptus*

L.A. hybrid lily
*Lilium*

Bear grass
*Xerophyllum*

Dusty miller
*Senecio*

Spray rose
*Rosa* 'Mimi Eden'

*Bouvardia* 'Diamond Pink'

Speedwell
*Veronica*

Sweet William
*Dianthus*

Bay leaf
*Laurus*

**Design Tip:** To form the purse, cut and fold in half a round piece of craft foam to form a semicircular pocket. Staple once at the center top. Create a handle by braiding three ribbons, and staple the ribbon braid to the sides of the craft foam purse. Starting at the outer edge, glue bay leaves onto the purse with floral adhesive, overlapping each leaf and subsequent rows, ending with a fan of leaves at the base of the purse.

California jasmine
*Jasminum*

23

Hybrid tea rose
*Rosa* 'Sanaa+'

Spray rose
*Rosa*

*Dianthus*, Gipsy group

Butcher's broom
*Ruscus*

Persian buttercup
*Ranunculus*

Hybrid tea rose
*Rosa* 'Bugatti'

Hybrid tea rose
*Rosa* 'Beauty by Oger'

French tulip
*Tulipa* 'Grand Style'

Sweet William
*Dianthus*

*Bouvardia*

Bay leaf
*Laurus*

**Design Tip:** Finish the hand-tied bouquet by wrapping the stems with wired ribbon. Create a detailed seam by scrunching a length of ribbon and securing it to the front of the stem bundle with pearl-headed corsage pins. To form the bay leaf collar, construct a garland of leaves with bullion wire, and wrap the garland around the edge of the bouquet.

Stock
*Matthiola*

Rose
*Rosa* 'Sweet Akito'

Persian buttercup
*Ranunculus*

Rose cockade
*Leucadendron tinctum*

Pepperberry
*Schinus*

Deciduous huckleberry
*Vaccinium*

Grampians *Thryptomene*
*Thryptomene calycina*

Thoroughwax
*Bupleurum*

Conebush
*Leucadendron terenifolia*

*Iris* foliage

*Cymbidium* 'Pontiac'

Hybrid tea rose
*Rosa* 'Hocus Pocus'

*Freesia*

Windflower
*Anemone*

Persian buttercup
*Ranunculus*

Persian buttercup
*Ranunculus*

**Design Tip:** To create this hand-tied bouquet, arrange flowers by hand in a traditional manner, and bind the stems with waterproof tape. Detail the binding point by wrapping with hot-pink wired ribbon. Secure the ribbon with a single corsage pin, and cut a "V" shape in the end of the single ribbon tail.

Miniature calla
*Zantedeschia* 'Red'

Hybrid tea rose
*Rosa* 'Black Baccara'

Pepperberry
*Schinus*

Persian buttercup
*Ranunculus*

Miniature *Cymbidium* 'Chailey Red'

*Sedum*

**Design Tip:** To create the "collar" surrounding this distinctive bouquet, bore a hole into the center of a shallow plastic design dish, insert a straight-handle bouquet holder through the hole, and adhere the bouquet holder to the dish with floral adhesive. Cover all exposed surfaces of the dish with fresh pepperberries, using floral adhesive. Arrange roses into the bouquet holder in a pavé manner, then arrange other floral materials atop the roses, creating a multidimensional bouquet.

Spray rose
*Rosa* 'Arrow Folies'

Hybrid tea rose
*Rosa* 'Black Magic'

Butcher's broom
*Ruscus*

Hybrid tea rose
*Rosa* 'Ruby Red'

**Design Tip:** To create the jeweled collar around the perimeter of this mixed red rose nosegay, arrange stems of *Ruscus* to form a collar beneath the roses on the underside of the bouquet, and weave the jewel garland through the stems of *Ruscus*.

Hybrid tea rose
*Rosa* 'Bulls Eye'

34

Hybrid tea rose
*Rosa* 'Black Magic'

Spider flower
*Grevillea*

Spray rose
*Rosa* 'Red Angel'

Parrot tulip
*Tulipa*

Persian buttercup
*Ranunculus*

Windflower
*Anemone*

*Eucalyptus* pods

Maidenhair fern
*Adiantum*

Hybrid tea rose
*Rosa* 'Black Baccara'

36

Hybrid tea rose
*Rosa* 'Bull's Eye'

*Bouvardia*

Conebush
*Leucadendron linifolium*

Nerve plant
*Fittonia*

Hybrid tea rose
*Rosa* 'Terracotta'

Spray rose
*Rosa* 'Tiramisu'

Pepperberry
*Schinus*

Hybrid tea rose
*Rosa* 'Morena'

*blue to lavender to violet*

*blue to lavender to violet*

Distinctive brides looking to make a vivid statement or classic brides seeking sophistication choose this color palette. From the cool ocean blues of a casual seaside resort to the majestic purples that impart a royal air, these colors lend an elegant aspect to any ceremony.

Grape hyacinth
*Muscari*

Hydrangea

**Design Tip:** Design this bouquet in a bouquet holder by first arranging *Hydrangea* blossoms in a tufted manner close to the surface of the bouquet holder's floral foam cage. The tightly tufted *Hydrangeas* provide a framework into which the *Muscaris* and stemmed *Stephanotises* can be securely arranged into the floral foam cage. *Stephanotises* can be stemmed quickly with chenille stems or Stephanotis Stems®.

Madagascar jasmine
*Stephanotis*

Madagascar jasmine
*Stephanotis*

Baby's breath
*Gypsophila*

**Design Tip:** Begin this bouquet by arranging a grower bunch of *Gypsophila* into a dense dome-shape nosegay. Bind and detail the stems with ribbon. Glue *Stephanotis* and *Delphinium* florets into the densely clustered *Gypsophila* with floral adhesive. The *Stephanotises* and *Delphinium* florets can be stemmed with chenille stems. Glue shortened pearl-headed corsage pins into the centers of the *Stephanotis* blossoms with floral adhesive.

Hybrid *Delphinium*

Grape hyacinth
*Muscari*

**Design Tip:** Design this bouquet in a bouquet holder by first arranging *Hydrangea* blossoms in a tufted manner close to the surface of the floral foam cage. Arrange *Muscaris* around the perimeter of the nosegay in several levels to create a fringy collar. Finish the bouquet by arranging discarded *Muscari* stems to create the illusion that they are intersecting the mound of *Hydrangeas*.

*Hydrangea*

50

Pincushion flower
*Scabiosa*

Rosemary
*Rosmarinus*

Deciduous huckleberry
*Vaccinium*

*Oxypetalum, Tweedia*

Sea holly
*Eryngium* 'Supernova'

Windflower
*Anemone*

Iris 'Telstar'

Scotch broom
*Cytisus*

Floss flower
*Ageratum*

Lavender
*Lavandula*

**Design Tip:** To create this unique bouquet, arrange six or more *Irises* and other florals in your hand, and surround the stems with inverted branches of Scotch broom. Bind with waterproof tape. Braid lengths of coordinating-colored ribbon, and wrap the Scotch broom "tail" with braided ribbon. Form the tail into a desired shape.

Speedwell
*Veronica*

Hybrid tea rose
*Rosa* 'Cool Water'

Hybrid *Delphinium*

Hyacinth
*Hyacinthus* 'Blue Pacific'

Waxflower
*Chamelaucium*

**Design Tip:** For the handle of this pomander bouquet, braid three lengths of ribbon, wire a wood pick to each end of the braid, and tape each pick with stem wrap to prevent the handle from wicking water. Secure each wood pick into the top of a dry floral foam sphere at a 45-degree angle with floral adhesive. Next, soak the floral foam sphere, insert two or three small picked-and-taped multiloop bows around the sphere, and arrange the flowers. Skewer hyacinth florets onto pearl-headed corsage pins, and tape chenille stems onto the pin ends to create stems. Add a few lengths of knotted ribbon, also wired to a wood pick and taped, at the bottom to form a tassel-like tail.

Spray rose
*Rosa* 'Special Sensation'

Hybrid tea rose
*Rosa* 'Blue Bird'

Waxflower
*Chamelaucium* 'Juriens Brook'

China aster
*Callistephus* 'Matsumoto' series

Prairie gentian
*Eustoma, Lisianthus* 'Mariachi' series

Dusty miller
*Senecio*

Spray rose
*Rosa* 'Pixie Folies'

Parrot tulip
*Tulipa*

Spray rose
*Rosa* 'Purple Sensation'

Dusty miller
*Senecio*

Stock
*Matthiola*

Hybrid tea rose
*Rosa* 'Delilah'

Hybrid tea rose
*Rosa* 'Aqua'

Hybrid tea rose
*Rosa* 'Mystery'

*Magnolia*

Hybrid tea rose
*Rosa* 'Purple Sensation'

**Design Tip:** Create this bouquet by arranging the roses and miniature callas in a spiral hand-tied manner, and bind the stems with waterproof tape. Next fashion a collar around the underside of the bouquet with *Magnolia* leaves, with their brown backsides facing upward, and bind again. Cover the binding point with coordinating ribbon.

Miniature calla
*Zantedeschia* 'Gem'

Heath
*Erica melanthera*

Hybrid tea rose
*Rosa* 'Mystery'

Scented-leaf geranium
*Pelargonium*

*Ruscus*

*Delphinium* Pacific Hybrid 'Mauve'

Hybrid tea rose
*Rosa* 'Stranger'

Fringed tulip
*Tulipa* 'Cummins'

Hybrid tea rose
*Rosa* 'Stranger'

Freesia

Bay leaf
*Laurus*

**Design Tip:** The pearl-studded, ribbon-wrapped handle on this bouquet is simple and fast to create. After completing the hand-tied bouquet and binding the stems with waterproof tape, wrap the stems with waterproof organza ribbon. To add the jeweled detail to the handle, insert coordinating-colored pearl-headed corsage pins upward into the stem bundle in an ordered pattern.

Stock
*Matthiola*

Moth orchid
*Phalaenopsis*

Kiwi vine
*Actinidia*

**Design Tip:** Wire two branches of kiwi vine together with aluminum wire to construct the form for this distinctive bouquet. Glue the *Phalaenopsis* orchids to the vine form with floral adhesive, with some of the orchids glued back to back, to create a bouquet that is attractive from all sides. String *Hypericum* berries randomly onto a length of metallic wire, and wrap artistically around the kiwi vine form.

St. John's wort, Tutsan
*Hypericum*

Miniature calla
*Zantedeschia* 'Gem'

Persian buttercup
*Ranunculus*

Kale
*Brassica*

Tree ivy berry
*Fatshedera*

Persian buttercup
*Ranunculus*

Tulip artichoke
*Cynara*

Persian buttercup
*Ranunculus*

70

Miniature calla
*Zantedeschia* 'Pillow Talk'

Persian buttercup
*Ranunculus*

Cattleya

Velvet plant
*Gynura*

Prairie gentian
*Eustoma, Lisianthus* 'Mariachi' series

Hyacinth
*Hyacinthus*

Stock
*Matthiola*

Miniature calla
*Zantedeschia* 'Lavender'

Persian buttercup
*Ranunculus*

Rose cone flower
*Isopogon*

Tulip artichoke
*Cynara*

Floss flower
*Ageratum*

Persian buttercup
*Ranunculus*

Conebush
*Leucadendron macowanii*

Nerve plant
*Fittonia* 'Red Anne'

Hybrid tea rose
*Rosa* 'Stranger'

Lilac
*Syringa*

Heath
*Erica*

Speedwell
*Veronica*

*Freesia*

**Design Tip:** Begin this hand-tied bouquet by clustering lilacs for the center. Arrange *Veronicas*, *Freesias*, *Ageratum* and heath around the lilac cluster to create a fringy collar of blossoms. Bind the stems with waterproof tape, and cover the binding with ribbon. Create an eight-loop "ribbon candy" bow with progressively smaller loops. Simultaneously secure the loops and attach the bow to the bouquet with a cluster of pearl-headed corsage pins.

Floss flower
*Ageratum*

Prairie gentian
*Eustoma, Lisianthus* 'Mariachi' series

Hyacinth
*Hyacinthus* 'Pacific Blue'

Statice
*Limonium*

Bay leaf
*Laurus*

**Design Tip:** To create the shower of florets over this monochromatic nosegay bouquet, which is designed in a bouquet holder, create several 18-inch-long strands of hyacinth florets by wrapping silver bullion wire two or three times around the base of each floret. Lay the blossom-laden wires over the top of the bouquet, securing them in place by tucking them into the bouquet at random intervals and wrapping them around some of the flowers in the nosegay.

China aster
*Callistephus* 'Matsumoto' series

# white to green to olive

*white to green to olive*

From the winter's snow to spring's budding foliage,

these colors are staples of the earth and whisper of

elegance and natural beauty. Representative of the

brand new life that couples are about to embark

upon, these crisp and verdant hues communicate

rebirth and renewal.

Calla
*Zantedeschia* 'Green Goddess'

**Design Tip:** To create the handle and collar for this nosegay, cut off the stems of several 'Green Goddess' standard callas, uncoil the blooms and remove the spadices. Glue the flattened calla blooms to the underside of a straight-handled bouquet holder with floral adhesive, covering the backside of the floral foam cage, to create the collar. Glue on an additional uncoiled calla with the stem intact, covering the bouquet holder handle and the bottoms of the callas that form the collar.

Double *Freesia*

Persian buttercup
*Ranunculus*

Windflower
*Anemone*

Tulip
*Tulipa*

Hybrid tea rose
*Rosa* 'Vendela'

Japhette orchid
*Cattleya*

Lily-of-the-valley
*Convallaria*

Hybrid tea rose
*Rosa* 'Talia'

Lilac
*Syringa*

Maidenhair fern
*Adiantum*

Sword fern
*Nephrolepis*

Seeded *Eucalyptus*

Hybrid tea rose
*Rosa* 'Avalanche'

Asiatic lily
*Lilium*

Prairie gentian
*Eustoma, Lisianthus*

Italian *Pittosporum*

Stock
*Matthiola*

French tulip
*Tulipa* 'Clearwater'

Transvaal daisy
*Gerbera*

Persian buttercup
*Ranunculus*

Hybrid tea rose
*Rosa* 'Akito'

Waxflower
*Chamelaucium* 'Albany Pearlflower'

Hybrid tea rose
*Rosa* 'Akito'

**Design Tip:** To begin this bouquet, secure a cluster of *Muscaris* by wrapping the base of their stems with waterproof tape. Cut a hole into the center of the floral foam cage of a bouquet holder. Glue the *Muscari* bundle into the hole with floral adhesive. Continue by arranging a row of roses around the base of the *Muscari* bundle. Fill in the rest of the bouquet with a ring of densely clustered white waxflower blossoms.

Grape hyacinth
*Muscari*

Hybrid tea rose
*Rosa* 'Super Green'

Spray rose
*Rosa* 'Snow Dance'

Conebush
*Leucadendron* 'Red Gem'

Tree ivy berry
*Fatshedera*

**Design Tip:** Adhere a plastic foam cone onto the top of a tussie-mussie holder with pan-melt glue. Cut off about one-third of the top part of the cone. Glue a small floral foam cage onto the flat top of the plastic foam cone with pan-melt glue. Cover the plastic-foam cone with rose petals using spray adhesive. Arrange flowers into the floral foam cage, and wrap the entire bouquet with a web of silver bullion wire. Add rhinestone pins into the center of the roses.

Kangaroo paw
*Anigozanthos*

Bells-of-Ireland
*Moluccella*

Dog eye
*Euphorbia*

Bishop's weed, Queen Anne's lace
*Ammi*

Lilac
*Syringa*

Star-of-Bethlehem
*Ornithogalum*

Madagascar jasmine
*Stephanotis*

Mullein
*Verbascum*

California jasmine
*Jasminum*

Grape hyacinth
*Muscari*

**Design Tip:** To form the purse's base, fold a rectangular piece of craft foam in half and staple the edges. Create a handle by braiding three lengths of ribbon, and staple the ribbon braid to the sides of the craft foam purse. Cover the purse with a *Verbascum* leaf on each side, gluing the leaves to the craft foam with floral adhesive. Fold the top of each leaf downward, and secure on each side with a pearl-headed corsage pin.

Wheat
*Triticum*

Freesia

Conebush
*Leucadendron linifolium*

**Design Tip:** To create the collar of wheat surrounding this bouquet, arrange individual stems of wheat around the perimeter of the floral foam cage of a bouquet holder at a downward angle. Dip the wheat stems first into floral adhesive to ensure they will stay in place. Arrange roses and *Freesias* into the floral foam cage, and add a row of *Leucadendron* cones between them and the wheat collar.

Hybrid tea rose
*Rosa* 'Escimo'

Pincushion flower
*Scabiosa 'Perfecta'*

California jasmine
*Jasminum*

Tulip
*Tulipa*

Waxflower
*Chamelaucium 'Albany Pearlflower'*

Windflower
*Anemone*

Bishop's weed, Queen Anne's lace
*Ammi*

Larkspur
*Delphinium, Consolida*

**Design Tip:** To create this hand-tied bouquet, arrange flowers in a traditional manner, and bind the stems with waterproof tape. Detail the binding point by wrapping it with frayed strips of craft mesh. Secure the mesh with nine pearl-headed corsage pins inserted into the stems in a square formation.

Speedwell
*Veronica*

Hybrid tea rose
*Rosa* 'Escimo'

Waxflower
*Eriostemon*

Prairie gentian
*Eustoma, Lisianthus*

Waxflower
*Chamelaucium* 'Sterling Range'

**Design Tip:** To make the cone-shaped handle for this bouquet, bind several inverted stems of waxflowers with silver bullion wire, and glue the bouquet holder handle into the cone-shaped bundle of waxflowers. To form the fringed collar of the bouquet, arrange short stems of waxflowers around the bottom edge of the bouquet holder's floral foam cage.

Windflower
*Anemone*

Wheat
*Triticum*

Bay leaf
*Laurus*

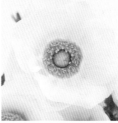

Windflower
*Anemone*

Windflower
*Anemone*

**Design Tip:** To create this bouquet's collar, attach either a prefabricated wire bouquet armature or a foam-centered board disc to the underside of a bouquet holder. Cover the collar with wheat by gluing wheat heads side by side around the collar with floral adhesive. Trim the wheat heads flush with the edge of the collar.

Prairie gentian
*Eustoma, Lisianthus*

*Hydrangea*

Salal
*Gaultheria*

**Design Tip:** Add "stems" to individual *Gardenia* blossoms with wood picks. Create the bouquet in a bouquet holder with the *Hydrangeas* and *Gardenias*, filling in with salal leaves. To create the cascading leaves, punch holes into individual salal leaves and attach them onto bullion wire, forming a garland. Attach wood picks to the garland, and secure them into the bouquet.

Cape jasmine
*Gardenia*

Lily grass
*Liriope*

**Design Tip:** Create a cascade of lily grass by combining several bunches and binding the stem ends with waterproof tape. Cover the tape with ribbon, and detail the wrapping with multicolored green, ivory and white pearl-headed corsage pins. Add *Stephanotis* blossoms by threading them onto the ends of the blades of the lily grass. Thread more than one blossom onto occasional blades of lily grass to create a fuller profusion of blossoms.

Madagascar jasmine
*Stephanotis*

Hybrid tea rose
*Rosa* 'Super Green'

*Iris* foliage

Bay leaf
*Laurus*

**Design Tip:** To create the conical handle, cover the base of an inverted plastic foam cone with *Iris* grass, attaching the grass to the cone with multicolored pearl-headed corsage pins. Hot-glue a floral foam cage atop the inverted cone in which to arrange the flowers. Create a handle by braiding three coordinating colors of ribbon and attaching the braid to the plastic foam cone with wood picks and hot glue.

Sea holly
*Eryngium* 'Supernova'

*Cattleya*

**Design Tip:** To begin this bouquet, gather three to four bunches of lily grass into a bundle. Create a handle for the bouquet by wrapping the ends of the lily grass stems with waterproof tape. Insert a straight-handle bouquet holder into the bound grass, then loop, fold and insert the grasses into the bouquet holder's floral foam cage. When the desired effect is achieved, arrange orchids into the floral foam cage.

Lily grass
*Liriope*

*cream to yellow to amber*

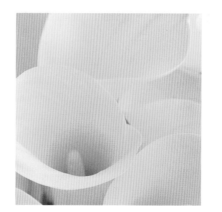 

*cream to yellow to amber*

No matter the weather, the sun is always shining on the bride on her special day. These golden hues bring the sun's full power to communicate the joy of the momentous occasion—from the dazzling liquid fire of amber to the understated but uplifting softness of cream.

Prairie gentian
*Eustoma, Lisianthus*

Spray rose
*Rosa* 'Limoncello'

Stock
*Matthiola*

Cattleya

**Design Tip:** To create the fringed collar of this bouquet, cut several circular pieces of craft mesh, allowing the edges to fray. Cut a hole into the center of each piece of mesh, and slip the mesh pieces over the top of the bouquet holder's floral foam cage, creating a flat collar of mesh around the point where the bouquet holder's foam cage ends and the plastic underside of the holder begins. Secure the mesh pieces in place by hot-gluing them to the base of the floral foam cage. Arrange orchids and *Freesias* into the floral foam cage.

Freesia

Asiatic lily
*Lilium*

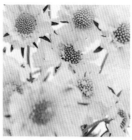

Pincushion flower
*Scabiosa*

Lily grass
*Liriope*

Windflower
*Anemone*

Bear grass
*Xerophyllum*

Australian willow myrtle
*Agonis* 'Red Southern Cross'

*Berzelia*

Scented leaf geranium
*Pelargonium*

Hybrid tea rose
*Rosa* 'Geneve'

Hybrid tea rose
*Rosa* 'Novia'

Conebush
*Leucadendron* 'Crown Jubilee'

**Design Tip:** Prepare roses for arrangement by wrapping the base of each rose head with decorative yarn, creating a soft fringed cocoon around each blossom. Arrange the roses into a bouquet holder. Cover the stem of the bouquet holder by gluing a feather-covered cone (available at a craft store) onto the base of the holder's floral foam cage. Randomly wrap the cone with the same yarn used on the roses to coordinate textures.

Tuberose
*Polianthes*

Hybrid tea rose
*Rosa* 'Novia'

*Hydrangea*

Hopbush
*Dodonaea*

Tuberose
*Polianthes*

**Design Tip:** To create the shower of tuberose florets and *Dodonaea* leaves over this monochromatic nosegay bouquet, which is designed in a bouquet holder, wrap the florets and leaves at random intervals along lengths of copper bullion wire. Lay the blossom- and leaf-laden wires over the top of the bouquet, securing them in place by tucking them into the bouquet at random intervals. To arrange individual tuberose florets into the nosegay, press colored pearl-headed corsage pins into the centers of the blossoms, tape chenille stems to the pin ends with stem wrap and insert them into the bouquet.

Hybrid tea rose
*Rosa* 'Geneve'

Hybrid tea rose
*Rosa* 'Limona'

Pincushion flower bud
*Scabiosa*

Spray rose
*Rosa* 'Sun City'

French tulip
*Tulipa* 'Akebono'

Sweetheart rose
*Rosa* 'Frisco'

Mini calla
*Zantedeschia* 'Lemon Drop'

Butcher's broom
*Ruscus*

Mini calla
*Zantedeschia* 'Mint Julep'

Persian buttercup
*Ranunculus*

Parrot tulip
*Tulipa* 'Salmon Parrot'

*Hydrangea*

Bay leaf
*Laurus*

Persian buttercup
*Ranunculus*

Daffodil, Jonquil
*Narcissus*

**Design Tip:** To give the stem-bundle handle of this hand-tied bouquet an elegant finish, first bind the stems with waterproof tape, then wrap them with waterproof organza ribbon. Detail the ribbon wrapping with a row of pearl-headed corsage pins, inserting each pin into the stem bundle at an upward angle, beginning at the top and working downward.

Hybrid tea rose
*Rosa* 'Ilios'

Spray rose
*Rosa* 'Limoncello'

**Design Tip:** To make a ribbon-covered collar, cut a doughnut-shaped piece of foam-centered board, and wrap it with ribbon. Hot-glue the ribbon-wrapped collar to the underside of the bouquet holder.

Spray rose
*Rosa* 'Sun City'

Hybrid tea rose
*Rosa* 'Citronella'

Bay leaf
*Laurus*

Finger *Acacia*

Miniature calla
*Zantedeschia*

French tulip
*Tulipa* 'La Courtine'

French parrot tulip
*Tulipa* 'Flaming Parrot'

**Design Tip:** Create this hand-tied cascading tulip bouquet by arranging French tulips in your hands to follow the natural curves of their stems. Bind the stems with waterproof tape, and cover the binding point with coordinating ribbon. To maintain the curvature of the stems, place a water-soaked terry-cloth towel over the top of the bouquet prior to refrigerated storage.

French tulip
*Tulipa* 'Mrs Scheepers'

Pincushion
*Leucospermum* 'High Gold'

Deciduous huckleberry
*Vaccinium*

**Design Tip:** To create the collar for this bouquet, arrange deciduous huckleberry around the base of the bouquet holder. Position each insertion so that the huckleberry creates a flat plane around the base of the floral foam cage. Trim the edges of the huckleberry with scissors. Arrange flowers into the floral foam cage. Encircle the bouquet with a "ribbon" of craft mesh that is cut into a strip with frayed edges.

Conebush
*Leucadendron* 'Lennox'

Miniature calla
*Zantedeschia* 'Flame'

Fern-leaf yarrow
*Achillea*

Conebush
*Leucadendron* 'Safari Sunset'

Kangaroo paw
*Anigozanthos*

**Design Tip:** To create the skirtlike collar for this nosegay, cut the stems off six to eight miniature callas, uncoil the blooms and remove the spadices. Invert the uncoiled calla blossoms, and glue them to the side of a bouquet holder's floral foam cage in an overlapping manner with floral adhesive. Arrange flowers into the floral foam cage.

Hybrid tea rose
*Rosa* 'Gypsy Curiosa'

Miniature sunflower
*Helianthus*

Conebush
*Leucadendron*

Throatwort
*Trachelium*

*Hydrangea*

St. John's wort, Tutsan
*Hypericum*

Rose cone flower
*Isopogon*

*Magnolia*

Miniature spider *Gerbera*

St. John's wort, Tutsan
*Hypericum*

Conebush
*Leucadendron* 'Red Eye'

*Cymbidium* 'Simplicity'

Conebush
*Leucadendron* 'Gold Strike'

Moon valley plant
*Pilea*

Tree ivy
*Fatshedera*

**Design Tip:** To create this unique pomander bouquet, glue tree-ivy leaves onto a dry floral foam sphere in an overlapping manner with floral adhesive. Create the handle and "cage" around the leaf-covered sphere with permanent vine. Soak the entire unit in water until the floral foam sphere is saturated. Arrange fresh floral materials into the top of the floral foam sphere.

*Berzelia*

*peach to orange to rust*

*peach to orange to rust*

Spicy but subtle, these citrus hues evoke an exotic aura. The bride who chooses colors in this family is bold but mysterious, approachable and energetic. Fun-loving and flirty, these colors easily transition from country to contemporary and reflect a couple's zest for life.

*Iris*

**Design Tip:** To transform this simple nosegay of roses and *Irises*, which can be designed in either a bouquet holder or as a hand-tied bouquet, into a cascade of organza ribbon and petals, fashion loops and streamers of wide organza ribbon, making some loops large enough to encircle the entire bouquet and encase the nosegay in a "cloud" of ribbon. Adhere rose petals to the ribbon with drops of floral adhesive.

Hybrid tea rose
*Rosa* 'Prima Donna'

Hybrid tea rose
*Rosa* 'Prima Donna'

Tulip
*Tulipa*

*Kunzea* 'Green Gold'

Sweetheart rose
*Rosa*

Spray rose
*Rosa* 'Cream Gracia'

Hybrid tea rose
*Rosa* 'Marmalade'

Transvaal daisy
Spider *Gerbera*

Seeded *Eucalyptus*

**Design Tip:** To create this diminutive hand-tied nosegay, arrange the flowers into the center of a prefabricated yarn-covered collar, and bind the stems with waterproof tape. Wrap the binding point and the entire length of the flower stems with coordinating yarn. Pin in a puff of metallic angel hair with pearl-headed corsage pins.

Hybrid tea rose
*Rosa* 'Milva'

Hybrid tea rose
*Rosa* 'Apricot'

Conebush
*Leucadendron macowanii*

L.A. hybrid lily
*Lilium*

**Design Tip:** Cut a square piece of craft mesh. Fold the corners in to the center, and staple them in place. Next, fold the corners in again, and staple in place again, creating a round shape. Cut a small hole into the center of the round piece of mesh, and place a straight-handle bouquet holder into the center of the mesh circle. Arrange the *Leucadendron* stems into the bouquet holder's floral foam cage through the mesh to hold it in place, then arrange the remainder of the flowers to complete the bouquet.

Pincushion
*Leucospermum* 'Spider'

Hybrid tea rose
*Rosa* 'Marmalade'

Transvaal daisy
Miniature spider *Gerbera*

Lily grass
*Liriope*

Bear grass
*Xerophyllum*

*Iris* foliage

Willow
*Salix*

**Design Tip:** Form the crescent-shaped armature for this bouquet with willow branches, and bind the stems with natural bind wire. Arrange flowers through the armature to create a spiral hand-tied bouquet. Bind the flower stems with waterproof tape, and cover the binding point with ribbon. Weave *Iris* foliage and lily grass through the armature.

Persian buttercup
*Ranunculus*

Parrot tulip
*Tulipa*

Pincushion flower pod
*Scabiosa*

Spider flower
*Grevillea*

Hybrid tea rose
*Rosa* 'Marie Claire'

Transvaal daisy
Miniature *Gerbera*

Sweetheart rose
*Rosa* 'Jade'

Persian buttercup
*Ranunculus*

English ivy
*Hedera*

Pot marigold
*Calendula*

160

Spray rose
*Rosa* 'Macarena'

Transvaal daisy
Spider *Gerbera*

St. John's wort, Tutsan
*Hypericum*

Willow
*Salix*

*Cymbidium* 'Carpinteria Sunrise'

Persian buttercup
*Ranunculus*

Hybrid tea rose
*Rosa* 'Wow'

**Design Tip:** Cover the handle of a bouquet holder with bundled willow tips, and bind them securely to the handle. Finish the bouquet by creating a garland of willow twigs attached to bullion wire and wrapping it around the outer edge of the bouquet.

Transvaal daisy
*Gerbera*

162

163

Sweetheart rose
*Rosa* 'Marina'

Pincushion
*Leucospermum* 'Sunrise'

Transvaal daisy
Miniature spider *Gerbera*

Seeded *Eucalyptus*

French tulip
*Tulipa* 'Avignon'

Glory lily
*Gloriosa*

Pepperberry
*Schinus*

Hybrid tea rose
*Rosa* 'Marie Claire'

Asiatic lily
*Lilium*

Baby's breath
*Gypsophila*

Transvaal daisy
*Gerbera*

Transvaal daisy
*Gerbera*

Salal
*Gaultheria*

**Design Tip:** Arrange a grower bunch of *Gypsophila* into a dense, mounded nosegay. Spray the surface of the nosegay with adhesive, and sprinkle on multicolored *Gerbera* petals. Gently pat the petals onto the surface of the mound of *Gypsophila*. Finish the underside of the bouquet by adding a collar of wired-and-taped salal leaves around the perimeter of the nosegay.

Transvaal daisy
*Gerbera*

Transvaal daisy
Miniature *Gerbera*

Persian buttercup
*Ranunculus*

Pincushion
*Leucospermum* 'California Sunset'

Persian buttercup
*Ranunculus*

St. John's wort, Tutsan
*Hypericum*

Lily grass
*Liriope*

Ivy
*Hedera*

**Design Tip:** To construct this dynamic "whirlpool"-style bouquet, roll a piece of square craft mesh into a tight cone and wrap the bottom three-fourths with copper metallic wire. Fan out the top portion of the mesh to create a collar for the bouquet. Glue a saturated straight-handle bouquet holder into the center of the mesh collar with pan-melt glue, and arrange the fresh flowers. To control the tulips' circular formation, wire the stems randomly to the mesh.

French tulip
*Tulipa* 'Menton'

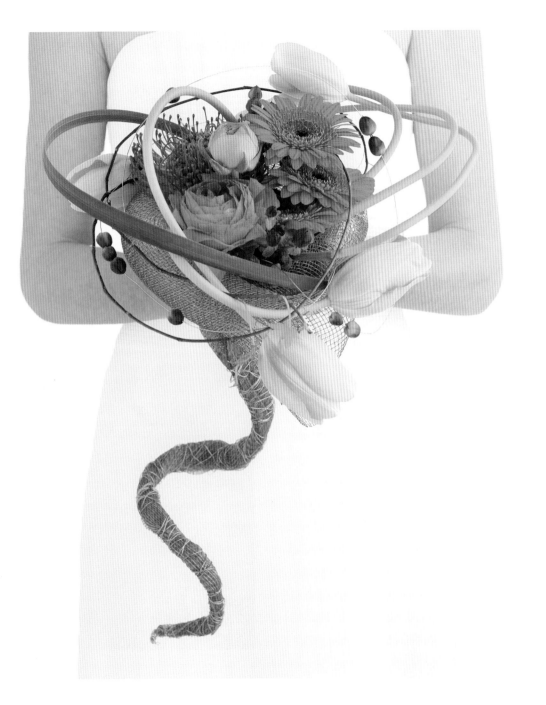

Transvaal daisy
Miniature *Gerbera*

Lily grass
*Liriope*

St. John's wort, Tutsan
*Hypericum*

Camellia

**Design Tip:** To create the copper aluminum wire armature, coil an entire package of wire around a dowel, leaving a small space between each coil. Remove the coil from the dowel, and form it into a square shape, creating the outer perimeter first and working inward in an "X"-shaped pattern. Continue until the square is filled in. Flatten the armature, and wrap copper bullion wire over the top of the armature. Arrange flower stems through the armature, and add more bullion wire over the top.

Persian buttercup
*Ranunculus*

170

*Cymbidium* 'Carpinteria Sunrise'

Bear grass
*Xerophyllum*

**Design Tip:** To create this contemporary pendulous bouquet, attach individual *Cymbidium* orchids and *Leucadendron* petals and leaves to lengths of copper bullion wire. Weave the wire around the throats and between the petals of the *Cymbidium* blooms so they hang upright, and pierce the *Leucadendron* leaves midway with the wire. Suspend the floral materials from a bundle of bamboo twigs beneath which blades of bear grass are wired to frame the dangling florals.

Conebush
*Leucadendron* 'Safari Sunset'

*Cymbidium* 'Carpinteria Surprise'

*Magnolia*

**Design Tip:** To construct this "directional" purse bouquet, cut the desired shape from two pieces of craft foam and secure the two pieces together with floral adhesive. Cover the outside of the purse with *Magnolia* leaves, backsides out, and trim them to the shape of the purse. To create the handle, wrap a heavy-gauge wire with yarn, and glue the handle to the purse with floral adhesive. Place a small piece of wet floral foam into the purse, and arrange the flowers.

Asiatic lily buds
*Lilium*

Hybrid tea rose
*Rosa* 'Black Beauty'

Fern-leaf yarrow
*Achillea*

Persian buttercup
*Ranunculus*

Glory lily
*Gloriosa*

Persian buttercup
*Ranunculus*

Steel grass
*Xanthorrhoea*

Hybrid tea rose
*Rosa* 'Hocus Pocus'

*Sedum*

Conebush
*Leucadendron* 'Jester'

Hybrid tea rose
*Rosa* 'Orange Appeal'

Tree fern
*Asparagus*

Conebush
*Leucadendron* 'Crown Jubilee'

**Design Tip:** Bundle two to three bunches of tree fern, binding the bundle of stems with waterproof tape. Trim the tree fern into a dome-shaped nosegay with scissors. Glue *Hypericum*, *Leucadendrons*, and permanent berries and leaves into the tree fern nosegay with floral adhesive. To finish the bouquet, place a thin layer of metallic angel hair over the top.

St. John's wort, Tutsan
*Hypericum*

*Cymbidium* 'Emily Joy'

Hopbush
*Dodonaea*

**Design Tip:** This elongated pomander bouquet requires that individual *Cymbidium* orchids be wired and taped so they can be assembled from the bottom up by wrapping the taped stems around each other. When all the orchids are in place, the *Leucadendrons* and *Dodonaea* can be glued in among the orchid blooms. These fillers also can be wired and taped, and inserted in tufts as the bouquet is assembled. To create a handle, add a ring of bark-covered wire at the top of the design.

Conebush
*Leucadendron* 'Crown Jubilee'

180

# Cut flower availability by season

SPRING

**Acacia**, Mimosa, Silver wattle
**Achillea**, Fern-leaf yarrow, Cottage yarrow
**Aconitum**, Monkshood
**Actinidia**, Kiwi
**Agapanthus**, African lily, Lily-of-the-Nile
**Ageratum**, Floss flower, Pussy foot
**Agrostemma**, Corn cockle
**Alchemilla**, Lady's mantle
**Allium**, Flowering onion, Flowering garlic
**Alstroemeria**, Peruvian lily, Inca lily
**Amaranthus**, Love-lies-bleeding, Tassel flower,
    Prince's feather
**Amaryllis**, Belladonna lily, Naked-lady lily
**Ammi**, Bishop's weed, Queen Anne's lace
**Anemone**, Windflower, Wind poppy
**Anigozanthos**, Kangaroo paw
**Anthurium**, Tail flower
**Antirrhinum**, Snapdragon
**Aquilegia**, Columbine
**Asclepias**, Butterfly weed
**Aster**, Heath aster, New York aster,
    Michaelmas daisy
**Astilbe**, False spiraea, Goat's beard
**Banksia**
**Boronia**
**Bouvardia**
**Brassica**, Flowering kale, Ornamental cabbage
**Buddleia**, Butterfly bush
**Bupleurum**, Thoroughwax
**Calendula**, Pot marigold
**Callistephus**, China aster
**Calluna**, Heather, Ling
**Campanula**, Bellflower, Canterbury bells
**Carthamus**, Safflower
**Cattleya**
**Celosia**, Cockscomb, Feathered amaranth,
    Plume *Celosia*
**Centaurea**, Cornflower, Bachelor's button
**Chaenomeles**, Flowering quince
**Chamelaucium**, Waxflower, Geraldton waxflower
**Chrysanthemum frutescens**, **Leucanthemum**,
    Marguerite daisy
**Cirsium**, Thistle, Plume thistle

**Clarkia**, **Godetia**, Satin flower,
    Farewell-to-spring
**Clivia**, Kaffir lily
**Convallaria**, Lily-of-the-valley
**Cosmos**, Mexican aster, Chocolate *Cosmos*
**Craspedia**, Billy button
**Crocosmia**, Montbretia
**Cymbidium**
**Cynara**, Artichoke, Globe artichoke, Cardoon
**Dahlia**
**Delphinium ajacis**, **Consolida**, Larkspur
**Delphinium**
**Dendranthema**, Chrysanthemum
**Dianthus**, Carnation, Miniature carnation,
    Sweet William, Gipsy
**Didiscus**, **Trachymene**, Blue lace flower
**Digitalis**, Foxglove
**Diosma**, **Coleonema**, Breath-of-heaven,
    Confetti bush
**Echinacea**, Purple coneflower
**Echinops**, Globe thistle
**Eremurus**, Desert candle, Foxtail lily
**Eryngium**, Sea holly
**Eucomis**, Pineapple lily
**Eustoma**, **Lisianthus**, Prairie gentian
**Forsythia**, Golden bells
**Freesia**
**Gardenia**, Cape jasmine
**Genista**, Broom
**Gerbera**, Transvaal daisy, African daisy
**Gladiolus**, Sword lily
**Gloriosa**, Glory lily
**Godetia**, **Clarkia**, Satin flower,
    Farewell-to-spring
**Gomphrena**, Globe amaranth
**Grevillea**, Spider flower
**Gypsophila**, Baby's breath
**Helenium**, Sneezeweed
**Helianthus**, Sunflower
**Helichrysum**, Strawflower
**Heliopsis**, Oxeye
**Hyacinthus**, Hyacinth
**Hydrangea**
**Hypericum**, St. John's wort, Tutsan
**Iberis**, Candytuft

**Iris**
**Isopogon**, Rose cone flower
**Lathyrus**, Sweet pea
**Lavandula**, Lavender
**Leptospermum**, Tea tree
**Leucadendron**, Conebush
**Leucospermum**, Pincushion
**Liatris**, Gay-feather, Blazing star
**Lilium**, Asiatic lily, Oriental lily, L.A. lily, O.T. lily,
    Easter lily
**Limonium**, Statice, Sea lavender, Caspia
**Lisianthus**, **Eustoma**, Prairie gentian
**Lysimachia**, Loosestrife
**Matricaria**, Feverfew
**Matthiola**, Stock, Gillyflower
**Moluccella**, Bells-of-Ireland
**Muscari**, Grape hyacinth
**Myosotis**, Forget-me-not
**Narcissus**, Daffodil, Jonquil, Paperwhite
**Nerine**, Guernsey lily
**Nigella**, Love-in-a-mist
**Ornithogalum**, Star-of-Bethlehem,
    Chincherinchee
**Ozothamnus**, Rice flower
**Paeonia**, Peony
**Papaver**, Poppy
**Pelargonium**, Geranium
**Phalaenopsis**, Moth orchid
**Phlox**
**Physostegia**, Obedience plant
**Polianthes**, Tuberose
**Protea**
**Prunus**, Plum, Cherry, Peach, Nectarine, Apricot
**Punica**, Pomegranate
**Ranunculus**, Persian buttercup
**Rosa**, Rose, Spray rose, Sweetheart rose
**Rosmarinus**, Rosemary
**Rudbeckia**, Black-eyed Susan
**Salix**, Willow
**Saponaria**, Soapwort
**Scabiosa**, Pincushion flower, Scabious
**Schinus**, Pepperberry, California pepper tree
**Scilla**, Squill, Blue bells, Wood hyacinth
**Solidago**, Goldenrod
**Solidaster**, Yellow aster

**Botanical name**, Common name

*Spiraea*

*Stephanotis*, Madagascar jasmine

*Strelitzia*, Bird-of-paradise

*Syringa*, Lilac

*Tagetes*, Marigold

*Thryptomene*, Grampians *Thryptomene*,
  Miniature waxflower

*Trachelium*, Throatwort

*Trachymene*, *Didiscus*, Blue lace flower

*Tulipa*, Tulip

*Veronica*, Speedwell

*Viburnum*, Snowball, Guelder rose

*Viola*, Sweet violet

*Watsonia*, Bugle lily

*Zantedeschia*, Calla, Miniature calla

*Zinnia*, Youth-and-old-age

SUMMER

*Acacia*, Mimosa, Silver wattle

*Achillea*, Fern-leaf yarrow, Cottage yarrow

*Aconitum*, Monkshood

*Actinidia*, Kiwi

*Agapanthus*, African lily, Lily-of-the-Nile

*Ageratum*, Floss flower, Pussy foot

*Agrostemma*, Corn cockle

*Alchemilla*, Lady's mantle

*Allium*, Flowering onion, Flowering garlic

*Alstroemeria*, Peruvian lily, Inca lily

*Amaranthus*, Love-lies-bleeding, Tassel flower,
  Prince's feather

*Amaryllis*, Belladonna lily, Naked-lady lily

*Ammi*, Bishop's weed, Queen Anne's lace

*Anemone*, Windflower, Wind poppy

*Anigozanthos*, Kangaroo paw

*Anthurium*, Tail flower

*Antirrhinum*, Snapdragon

*Asclepias*, Butterfly weed

*Aster*, Heath aster, New York aster,
  Michaelmas daisy

*Astilbe*, False spiraea, Goat's beard

*Banksia*

*Boronia*

*Bouvardia*

*Brassica*, Flowering kale, Ornamental cabbage

*Buddleia*, Butterfly bush

*Bupleurum*, Thoroughwax

*Calendula*, Pot marigold

*Callistephus*, China aster

*Calluna*, Heather, Ling

*Campanula*, Bellflower, Canterbury bells

*Capsicum*, Ornamental pepper

*Carthamus*, Safflower

*Cattleya*

*Celosia*, Cockscomb, Feathered amaranth,
  Plume *Celosia*

*Centaurea*, Cornflower, Bachelor's button

*Chamelaucium*, Waxflower, Geraldton waxflower

*Chelone*, Turtle head, Snake head

*Chrysanthemum frutescens*, *Leucanthemum*,
  Marguerite daisy

*Cirsium*, Thistle, Plume thistle

*Clarkia*, *Godetia*, Satin flower,
  Farewell-to-spring

*Convallaria*, Lily-of-the-valley

*Cosmos*, Mexican aster, Chocolate *Cosmos*

*Craspedia*, Billy button

*Crocosmia*, Montbretia

*Cymbidium*

*Cynara*, Artichoke, Globe artichoke, Cardoon

*Dahlia*

*Delphinium ajacis*, *Consolida*, Larkspur

*Delphinium*

*Dendranthema*, Chrysanthemum

*Dianthus*, Carnation, Miniature carnation,
  Sweet William, Gipsy

*Didiscus*, *Trachymene*, Blue lace flower

*Digitalis*, Foxglove

*Echinacea*, Purple coneflower

*Echinops*, Globe thistle

*Eremurus*, Desert candle, Foxtail lily

*Eriostemon*, Wax flower

*Eryngium*, Sea holly

*Eucomis*, Pineapple lily

*Eupatorium*, Joe Pye weed, Hemp agrimony

*Eustoma*, *Lisianthus*, Prairie gentian

*Freesia*

*Gardenia*, Cape jasmine

*Gerbera*, Transvaal daisy, African daisy

*Gladiolus*, Sword lily

*Gloriosa*, Glory lily

*Godetia*, *Clarkia*, Satin flower,
  Farewell-to-spring

*Gomphrena*, Globe amaranth

*Grevillea*, Spider flower

*Gypsophila*, Baby's breath

*Helenium*, Sneezeweed

*Helianthus*, Sunflower

*Helichrysum*, Strawflower

*Heliopsis*, Oxeye

*Hippeastrum*, Amaryllis, Barbados lily

*Hyacinthus*, Hyacinth

*Hydrangea*

*Hypericum*, St. John's wort, Tutsan

*Iberis*, Candytuft

*Iris*

*Lathyrus*, Sweet pea

*Lavandula*, Lavender

*Leptospermum*, Tea tree

*Leucadendron*, Conebush

*Leucospermum*, Pincushion

*Liatris*, Gay-feather, Blazing star

*Lilium*, Asiatic lily, Oriental lily, L.A. lily, O.T. lily,
  Easter lily

*Limonium*, Statice, Sea lavender, Caspia

*Lisianthus*, *Eustoma*, Prairie gentian

*Lysimachia*, Loosestrife

*Matricaria*, Feverfew

*Matthiola*, Stock, Gillyflower

*Moluccella*, Bells-of-Ireland

*Monarda*, Bee balm, Oswego tea

*Myosotis*, Forget-me-not

*Nerine*, Guernsey lily

*Nigella*, Love-in-a-mist

*Ornithogalum*, Star-of-Bethlehem,
  Chincherinchee

*Ozothamnus*, Rice flower

*Paeonia*, Peony

*Papaver*, Poppy

*Pelargonium*, Geranium

*Phalaenopsis*, Moth orchid

*Phlox*

*Physalis*, Chinese lantern

*Physostegia*, Obedience plant

*Polianthes*, Tuberose

*Protea*

*Punica*, Pomegranate

*Ranunculus*, Persian buttercup

*Rosa*, Rose, Spray rose, Sweetheart rose

*Rosmarinus*, Rosemary

*Rudbeckia*, Black-eyed Susan

*Salix*, Willow

*Saponaria*, Soapwort

*Scabiosa*, Pincushion flower, Scabious

*Schinus*, Pepperberry, California pepper tree

*Sedum*, Stonecrop

*Solidago*, Goldenrod

*Solidaster*, Yellow aster

*Botanical name*, Common name    183

*Spiraea*

*Stephanotis*, Madagascar jasmine

*Strelitzia*, Bird-of-paradise

*Symphoricarpos*, Snowberry

*Syringa*, Lilac

*Tagetes*, Marigold

*Thryptomene*, Grampians *Thryptomene*,
Miniature waxflower

*Trachelium*, Throatwort

*Trachymene*, *Didiscus*, Blue lace flower

*Tulipa*, Tulip

*Typha*, Cattail

*Veronica*, Speedwell

*Viola*, Sweet violet

*Watsonia*, Bugle lily

*Zantedeschia*, Calla, Miniature calla

*Zinnia*, Youth-and-old-age

AUTUMN

*Acacia*, Mimosa, Silver wattle

*Achillea*, Fern-leaf yarrow, Cottage yarrow

*Aconitum*, Monkshood

*Actinidia*, Kiwi

*Agapanthus*, African lily, Lily-of-the-Nile

*Ageratum*, Floss flower, Pussy foot

*Allium*, Flowering onion, Flowering garlic

*Alstroemeria*, Peruvian lily, Inca lily

*Amaranthus*, Love-lies-bleeding, Tassel flower,
Prince's feather

*Ammi*, Bishop's weed, Queen Anne's lace

*Anemone*, Windflower, Wind poppy

*Anigozanthos*, Kangaroo paw

*Anthurium*, Tail flower

*Antirrhinum*, Snapdragon

*Asclepias*, Butterfly weed

*Aster*, Heath aster, New York aster,
Michaelmas daisy

*Banksia*

*Boronia*

*Bouvardia*

*Brassica*, Flowering kale, Ornamental cabbage

*Buddleia*, Butterfly bush

*Bupleurum*, Thoroughwax

*Calendula*, Pot marigold

*Callicarpa*, Beautyberry, French mulberry

*Callistephus*, China aster

*Calluna*, Heather, Scotch heather, Ling

*Campanula*, Bellflower, Canterbury bells

*Capsicum*, Ornamental pepper

*Carthamus*, Safflower

*Cattleya*

*Celosia*, Cockscomb, Feathered amaranth,
Plume *Celosia*

*Centaurea*, Cornflower, Bachelor's button

*Chaenomeles*, Flowering quince

*Chamelaucium*, Waxflower, Geraldton waxflower

*Chrysanthemum frutescens*, *Leucanthemum*,
Marguerite daisy

*Cirsium*, Thistle, Plume thistle

*Clarkia*, *Godetia*, Satin flower,
Farewell-to-spring

*Coleonema*, *Diosma*, Confetti bush,
Breath-of-heaven

*Convallaria*, Lily-of-the-valley

*Cosmos* Mexican aster, Chocolate *Cosmos*

*Craspedia*, Billy button

*Crocosmia*, Montbretia

*Cymbidium*

*Cynara*, Artichoke, Globe artichoke, Cardoon

*Dahlia*

*Delphinium ajacis*, *Consolida*, Larkspur

*Delphinium*

*Dendranthema*, Chrysanthemum

*Dianthus*, Carnation, Miniature carnation,
Sweet William, Gipsy

*Didiscus*, *Trachymene*, Blue lace flower

*Digitalis*, Foxglove

*Echinacea*, Purple coneflower

*Echinops*, Globe thistle

*Erica*, Heath

*Eriostemon*, Wax flower

*Eryngium*, Sea holly

*Eustoma*, *Lisianthus*, Prairie gentian

*Forsythia*, Golden bells

*Freesia*

*Gardenia*, Cape jasmine

*Gerbera*, Transvaal daisy, African daisy

*Gladiolus*, Sword lily

*Gloriosa*, Glory lily

*Godetia*, *Clarkia*, Satin flower,
Farewell-to-spring

*Gomphrena*, Globe amaranth

*Grevillea*, Spider flower

*Gypsophila*, Baby's breath

*Helenium*, Sneezeweed

*Helianthus*, Sunflower

*Helichrysum*, Strawflower

*Hippeastrum*, Amaryllis, Barbados lily

*Hydrangea*

*Hypericum*, St. John's wort, Tutsan

*Iberis*, Candytuft

*Iris*

*Lathyrus*, Sweet pea

*Lavandula*, Lavender

*Leptospermum*, Tea tree

*Leucadendron*, Conebush

*Leucospermum*, Pincushion

*Liatris*, Gay-feather, Blazing star

*Lilium*, Asiatic lily, Oriental lily, L.A. lily, O.T. lily,
Easter lily

*Limonium*, Statice, Sea lavender, Caspia

*Lisianthus*, *Eustoma*, Prairie gentian

*Lysimachia*, Loosestrife

*Matricaria*, Feverfew

*Matthiola*, Stock, Gillyflower

*Moluccella*, Bells-of-Ireland

*Monarda*, Bee balm, Oswego tea

*Myosotis*, Forget-me-not

*Narcissus*, Paperwhite

*Nerine*, Guernsey lily

*Nigella*, Love-in-a-mist

*Ornithogalum*, Star-of-Bethlehem,
Chincherinchee

*Ozothamnus*, Rice flower

*Papaver*, Poppy

*Pelargonium*, Geranium

*Phalaenopsis*, Moth orchid

*Phlox*

*Physalis*, Chinese lantern

*Physostegia*, Obedience plant

*Polianthes*, Tuberose

*Protea*

*Punica*, Pomegranate

*Ranunculus*, Persian buttercup

*Rosa*, Rose, Spray rose, Sweetheart rose

*Rosmarinus*, Rosemary

*Rudbeckia*, Black-eyed Susan

*Salix*, Willow

*Saponaria*, Soapwort

*Scabiosa*, Pincushion flower, Scabious

*Schinus*, Pepperberry, California pepper tree

*Sedum*, Stonecrop

*Solidago*, Goldenrod

*Solidaster*, Yellow aster

*Spiraea*

*Stephanotis*, Madagascar jasmine

*Strelitzia*, Bird-of-paradise

*Symphoricarpos*, Snowberry
*Syringa*, Lilac
*Tagetes*, Marigold
*Thryptomene*, Grampians *Thryptomene*,
  Miniature waxflower
*Trachelium*, Throatwort
*Trachymene*, *Didiscus*, Blue lace flower
*Tulipa*, Tulip
*Typha*, Cattail
*Veronica*, Speedwell
*Viola*, Sweet violet
*Zantedeschia*, Calla, Miniature calla
*Zinnia*, Youth-and-old-age

WINTER

*Acacia*, Mimosa, Silver wattle
*Achillea*, Fern-leaf yarrow, Cottage yarrow
*Aconitum*, Monkshood
*Actinidia*, Kiwi
*Allium*, Flowering onion, Flowering garlic
*Alstroemeria*, Peruvian lily, Inca lily
*Amaranthus hypochondriacus*, Prince's feather
*Ammi*, Bishop's weed, Queen Anne's lace
*Anemone*, Windflower, Wind poppy
*Anigozanthos*, Kangaroo paw
*Anthurium*, Tail flower
*Antirrhinum*, Snapdragon
*Aquilegia*, Columbine
*Asclepias*, Butterfly weed
*Aster*, Heath aster, New York aster,
  Michaelmas daisy
*Banksia*
*Boronia*
*Bouvardia*
*Brassica*, Flowering kale, Ornamental cabbage
*Bupleurum*, Thoroughwax
*Calendula*, Pot marigold
*Callicarpa*, Beautyberry, French mulberry
*Callistephus*, China aster
*Calluna*, Heather, Ling
*Campanula*, Bellflower, Canterbury bells
*Cattleya*
*Centaurea*, Cornflower, Bachelor's button
*Chaenomeles*, Flowering quince
*Chamelaucium*, Waxflower, Geraldton waxflower
*Chrysanthemum frutescens*, *Leucanthemum*,
  Marguerite daisy
*Cirsium*, Thistle, Plume thistle

*Clarkia*, *Godetia*, Satin flower,
  Farewell-to-spring
*Clivia*, Kaffir lily
*Coleonema*, *Diosma*, Confetti bush,
  Breath-of-heaven
*Convallaria*, Lily-of-the-valley
*Craspedia*, Billy button
*Crocosmia*, Montbretia
*Cymbidium*
*Cynara*, Artichoke, Globe artichoke, Cardoon
*Dahlia*
*Delphinium ajacis*, *Consolida*, Larkspur
*Delphinium*
*Dendranthema*, Chrysanthemum
*Dianthus*, Carnation, Miniature carnation,
  Sweet William, Gipsy
*Didiscus*, *Trachymene*, Blue lace flower
*Digitalis*, Foxglove
*Diosma*, *Coleonema*, Breath-of-heaven,
  Confetti bush
*Echinops*, Globe thistle
*Eremurus*, Desert candle, Foxtail lily
*Erica*, Heath
*Eriostemon*, Wax flower
*Eryngium*, Sea holly
*Eustoma*, *Lisianthus*, Prairie gentian
*Forsythia*, Golden bells
*Freesia*
*Gardenia*, Cape jasmine
*Genista*, Broom
*Gerbera*, Transvaal daisy, African daisy
*Gladiolus*, Sword lily
*Gloriosa*, Glory lily
*Godetia*, *Clarkia*, Satin flower,
  Farewell-to-spring
*Grevillea*, Spider flower
*Gypsophila*, Baby's breath
*Helianthus*, Sunflower
*Hippeastrum*, Amaryllis, Barbados lily
*Hyacinthus*, Hyacinth
*Hydrangea*
*Hypericum*, St. John's wort, Tutsan
*Iberis*, Candytuft
*Iris*
*Isopogon*, Rose cone flower
*Lathyrus*, Sweet pea
*Lavandula*, Lavender
*Leptospermum*, Tea tree
*Leucadendron*, Conebush

*Leucospermum*, Pincushion
*Liatris*, Gay-feather, Blazing star
*Lilium*, Asiatic lily, Oriental lily, L.A. lily, O.T. lily,
  Easter lily
*Limonium*, Statice, Sea lavender, Caspia
*Lisianthus*, *Eustoma*, Prairie gentian
*Lysimachia*, Loosestrife
*Matthiola*, Stock, Gillyflower
*Moluccella*, Bells-of-Ireland
*Muscari*, Grape hyacinth
*Myosotis*, Forget-me-not
*Narcissus*, Daffodil, Jonquil, Paperwhite
*Nerine*, Guernsey lily
*Ornithogalum*, Star-of-Bethlehem,
  Chincherinchee
*Ozothamnus*, Rice flower
*Papaver*, Poppy
*Pelargonium*, Geranium
*Phalaenopsis*, Moth orchid
*Phlox*
*Polianthes*, Tuberose
*Protea*
*Prunus*, Plum, Cherry, Peach, Nectarine, Apricot
*Ranunculus*, Persian buttercup
*Rosa*, Rose, Spray rose, Sweetheart rose
*Rosmarinus*, Rosemary
*Rudbeckia*, Black-eyed Susan
*Salix*, Willow
*Saponaria*, Soapwort
*Scabiosa*, Pincushion flower, Scabious
*Schinus*, Pepperberry, California pepper tree
*Scilla*, Squill, Blue bells, Wood hyacinth
*Solidago*, Goldenrod
*Solidaster*, Yellow aster
*Spiraea*
*Stephanotis*, Madagascar jasmine
*Strelitzia*, Bird-of-paradise
*Syringa*, Lilac
*Thryptomene*, Grampians *Thryptomene*,
  Miniature waxflower
*Trachelium*, Throatwort
*Trachymene*, *Didiscus*, Blue lace flower
*Tulipa*, Tulip
*Veronica*, Speedwell
*Viburnum*, Snowball, Guelder rose
*Viola*, Sweet violet
*Watsonia*, Bugle lily
*Zantedeschia*, Calla, Miniature calla

*Botanical name*, Common name   185

# Cut flower availability by color

**Botanical name**, Common name    187

***Asclepias***, Butterfly weed
***Astilbe***, False spiraea, Goat's beard
***Banksia***
***Buddleia***, Butterfly bush
***Capsicum***, Ornamental pepper
***Celosia***, Cockscomb, Feathered amaranth,
   Plume *Celosia*
***Centaurea***, Globe cornflower, Salton
***Chrysanthemum frutescens***, ***Leucanthemum***,
   Marguerite daisy
***Cosmos***, Mexican aster
***Craspedia***, Billy button
***Cymbidium***
***Dahlia***
***Dendranthema***, Chrysanthemum
***Dianthus***, Carnation, Miniature carnation,
   Sweet William, Gipsy
***Digitalis***, Foxglove
***Eremurus***, Desert candle, Foxtail lily
***Forsythia***, Golden bells
***Freesia***
***Genista***, Broom
***Gerbera***, Transvaal daisy, African daisy
***Gladiolus***, Sword lily
***Gomphrena***, Globe amaranth
***Helenium***, Sneezeweed
***Helianthus***, Sunflower
***Helichrysum***, Strawflower
***Heliopsis***, Oxeye
***Hyacinthus***, Hyacinth
***Iris***
***Isopogon***, Rose cone flower
***Lathyrus***, Sweet pea
***Leucadendron***, Conebush
***Leucospermum***, Pincushion
***Lilium***, Asiatic lily, Oriental lily, L.A. lily, O.T. lily,
   Easter lily
***Limonium***, Statice, Sea lavender, Caspia
***Lysimachia***, Loosestrife
***Matricaria***, Feverfew
***Matthiola***, Stock, Gillyflower
***Narcissus***, Daffodil, Jonquil, Paperwhite
***Ornithogalum***, Star-of-Bethlehem
***Ozothamnus***, Rice flower
***Paeonia***, Peony
***Papaver***, Poppy
***Polianthes***, Tuberose
***Protea***
***Ranunculus***, Persian buttercup

***Rosa***, Rose, Spray rose, Sweetheart rose
***Rudbeckia***, Black-eyed Susan
***Solidago***, Goldenrod
***Solidaster***, Yellow aster
***Tagetes***, Marigold
***Tulipa***, Tulip
***Viburnum***, Snowball, Guelder rose
***Zantedeschia***, Calla, Miniature calla
***Zinnia***, Youth-and-old-age

PINK TO RED TO BURGUNDY
***Achillea***, Cottage yarrow
***Agrostemma***, Corn cockle
***Alstroemeria***, Peruvian lily, Inca lily
***Amaranthus***, Love-lies-bleeding, Tassel flower,
   Prince's feather
***Amaryllis***, Belladonna lily, Naked-lady lily
***Anemone***, Windflower, Wind poppy
***Anigozanthos***, Kangaroo paw
***Anthurium***, Tail flower
***Antirrhinum***, Snapdragon
***Aquilegia***, Columbine
***Asclepias***, Butterfly weed
***Astilbe***, False spiraea, Goat's beard
***Bouvardia***
***Brassica***, Flowering kale, Ornamental cabbage
***Buddleia***, Butterfly bush
***Callistephus***, China aster
***Campanula***, Bellflower, Canterbury bells
***Centaurea***, Cornflower, Bachelor's button
***Chaenomeles***, Flowering quince
***Chamelaucium***, Waxflower, Geraldton waxflower
***Chelone***, Turtle head, Snake head
***Cirsium***, Thistle, Plume thistle
***Clarkia***, ***Godetia***, Satin flower,
   Farewell-to-spring
***Coleonema***, ***Diosma***, Confetti bush,
   Breath-of-heaven
***Cosmos***, Mexican aster, Chocolate *Cosmos*
***Cymbidium***
***Dahlia***
***Delphinium ajacis***, ***Consolida***, Larkspur
***Delphinium***
***Dendranthema***, Chrysanthemum
***Dianthus***, Carnation, Miniature carnation,
   Sweet William, Gipsy
***Digitalis***, Foxglove
***Diosma***, ***Coleonema***, Breath-of-heaven,
   Confetti bush

***Eremurus***, Desert candle, Foxtail lily
***Eriostemon***, Wax flower
***Eucomis***, Pineapple lily
***Eupatorium***, Joe Pye weed, Hemp agrimony
***Eustoma***, ***Lisianthus***, Prairie gentian
***Freesia***
***Genista***, Broom
***Gerbera***, Transvaal daisy, African daisy
***Gladiolus***, Sword lily
***Gloriosa***, Glory lily
***Godetia***, ***Clarkia***, Satin flower,
   Farewell-to-spring
***Gomphrena***, Globe amaranth
***Grevillea***, Spider flower
***Gypsophila***, Baby's breath
***Helichrysum***, Strawflower
***Hippeastrum***, Amaryllis, Barbados lily
***Hyacinthus***, Hyacinth
***Hydrangea***
***Hypericum***, St. John's wort, Tutsan
***Lathyrus***, Sweet pea
***Leptospermum***, Tea tree
***Leucadendron***, Conebush
***Lilium***, Asiatic lily, Oriental lily, L.A. lily, O.T. lily,
   Easter lily
***Limonium***, Statice, Sea lavender, Caspia
***Lisianthus***, ***Eustoma***, Prairie gentian
***Matthiola***, Stock, Gillyflower
***Monarda***, Bee balm, Oswego tea
***Myosotis***, Forget-me-not
***Nerine***, Guernsey lily
***Paeonia***, Peony
***Papaver***, Poppy
***Pelargonium***, Geranium
***Phlox***
***Protea***
***Prunus***, Plum, Cherry, Peach, Nectarine, Apricot
***Punica***, Pomegranate
***Ranunculus***, Persian buttercup
***Rosa***, Rose, Spray rose, Sweetheart rose
***Saponaria***, Soapwort
***Scabiosa***, Pincushion flower, Scabious
***Schinus***, Pepperberry, California pepper tree
***Sedum***, Stonecrop
***Symphoricarpos***, Snowberry
***Syringa***, Lilac
***Thryptomene***, Grampians *Thryptomene*,
   Miniature waxflower
***Trachelium***, Throatwort

*Tulipa*, Tulip
*Watsonia*, Bugle lily
*Zantedeschia*, Calla, Miniature calla
*Zinnia*, Youth-and-old-age

PEACH TO ORANGE TO RUST
*Achillea*, Cottage yarrow
*Alstroemeria*, Peruvian lily, Inca lily
*Anthurium*, Tail flower
*Antirrhinum*, Snapdragon
*Aquilegia*, Columbine
*Asclepias*, Butterfly weed
*Banksia*
*Buddleia*, Butterfly bush
*Calendula*, Pot marigold
*Capsicum*, Ornamental pepper
*Carthamus*, Safflower
*Celosia*, Cockscomb, Feathered amaranth,
   Plume *Celosia*
*Chaenomeles*, Flowering quince
*Clarkia*, *Godetia*, Satin flower,
   Farewell-to-spring
*Clivia*, Kaffir lily
*Cosmos*, Mexican aster
*Crocosmia*, Montbretia
*Cymbidium*
*Dahlia*
*Delphinium ajacis*, *Consolida*, Larkspur
*Dendranthema*, Chrysanthemum
*Dianthus*, Carnation, Miniature carnation,
   Sweet William, Gipsy
*Eucomis*, Pineapple lily
*Freesia*
*Genista*, Broom
*Gerbera*, Transvaal daisy, African daisy
*Gladiolus*, Sword lily
*Godetia*, *Clarkia*, Satin flower,
   Farewell-to-spring
*Gomphrena*, Globe amaranth
*Grevillea*, Spider flower
*Helenium*, Sneezeweed
*Helianthus*, Sunflower
*Helichrysum*, Strawflower
*Hippeastrum*, Amaryllis, Barbados lily
*Hyacinthus*, Hyacinth
*Hypericum*, St. John's wort, Tutsan
*Lathyrus*, Sweet pea
*Leucadendron*, Conebush
*Leucospermum*, Pincushion

*Lilium*, Asiatic lily, Oriental lily, L.A. lily, O.T. lily,
   Easter lily
*Limonium*, Statice
*Lisianthus*, *Eustoma*, Prairie gentian
*Matthiola*, Stock, Gillyflower
*Narcissus*, Daffodil, Jonquil, Paperwhite
*Paeonia*, Peony
*Papaver*, Poppy
*Pelargonium*, Geranium
*Physalis*, Chinese lantern
*Prunus*, Plum, Cherry, Peach, Nectarine, Apricot
*Ranunculus*, Persian buttercup
*Rosa*, Rose, Spray rose, Sweetheart rose
*Rudbeckia*, Black-eyed Susan
*Strelitzia*, Bird-of-paradise
*Tagetes*, Marigold
*Tulipa*, Tulip
*Watsonia*, Bugle lily
*Zantedeschia*, Calla, Miniature calla
*Zinnia*, Youth-and-old-age

BLUE TO LAVENDER TO VIOLET
*Aconitum*, Monkshood
*Agapanthus*, African lily, Lily-of-the-Nile
*Ageratum*, Floss flower, Pussy foot
*Allium*, Flowering onion, Flowering garlic
*Alstroemeria*, Peruvian lily, Inca lily
*Anemone*, Windflower, Wind poppy
*Antirrhinum*, Snapdragon
*Aquilegia*, Columbine
*Aster*, New York aster, Michaelmas daisy
*Boronia*
*Brassica*, Flowering kale, Ornamental cabbage
*Brodiaea*, *Triteleia*
*Buddleia*, Butterfly bush
*Callicarpa*, Beautyberry, French mulberry
*Callistephus*, China aster
*Calluna*, Heather, Ling
*Campanula*, Bellflower, Canterbury bells
*Cattleya*
*Celosia*, Cockscomb, Feathered amaranth,
   Plume *Celosia*
*Centaurea*, Cornflower, Bachelor's button
*Chamelaucium*, Waxflower, Geraldton waxflower
*Chelone*, Turtle head, Snake head
*Cirsium*, Thistle, Plume thistle
*Cosmos*, Mexican aster
*Cymbidium*
*Cynara*, Tulip artichoke

*Dahlia*
*Delphinium ajacis*, *Consolida*, Larkspur
*Delphinium*
*Dendranthema*, Chrysanthemum
*Dianthus*, Carnation, Miniature carnation,
   Sweet William, Gipsy
*Didiscus*, *Trachymene*, Blue lace flower
*Digitalis*, Foxglove
*Echinacea*, Purple coneflower
*Echinops*, Globe thistle
*Erica*, Heath
*Eryngium*, Sea holly
*Eupatorium*, Joe Pye weed, Hemp agrimony
*Eustoma*, *Lisianthus*, Prairie gentian
*Freesia*
*Genista*, Broom
*Gladiolus*, Sword lily
*Gomphrena*, Globe amaranth
*Helichrysum*, Strawflower
*Hyacinthus*, Hyacinth
*Hydrangea*
*Iris*
*Isopogon*, Rose cone flower
*Lathyrus*, Sweet pea
*Lavandula*, Lavender
*Liatris*, Gay-feather, Blazing star
*Limonium*, Statice, Sea lavender, Caspia
*Lisianthus*, *Eustoma*, Prairie gentian
*Matthiola*, Stock, Gillyflower
*Muscari*, Grape hyacinth
*Myosotis*, Forget-me-not
*Nigella*, Love-in-a-mist
*Phalaenopsis*, Moth orchid
*Phlox*
*Physostegia*, Obedience plant
*Ranunculus*, Persian buttercup
*Rosa*, Rose, Spray rose, Sweetheart rose
*Scabiosa*, Pincushion flower, Scabious
*Scilla*, Squill, Blue bells, Wood hyacinth
*Syringa*, Lilac
*Trachelium*, Throatwort
*Trachymene*, *Didiscus*, Blue lace flower
*Tulipa*, Tulip
*Veronica*, Speedwell
*Viola*, Sweet violet
*Zantedeschia*, Calla, Miniature calla
*Zinnia*, Youth-and-old-age

# Cut flower and foliage growers

All fresh cut flowers and foliages featured in this book were provided by the following grower members of the **California Cut Flower Commission (CCFC)**. For more information about the growers' products, contact the growers at the phone numbers and through the Web sites listed below, or contact your favorite wholesaler. You can also visit the CCFC's Web site at *www.ccfc.org*.

**AMERI-CAL FLORAL**
Watsonville, California
800.322.6529 / 831.728.4205
*www.ameri-cal.com*

**B&H FLOWERS, INC.**
Carpinteria, California
800.682.5666 / 805.684.4550
*www.bandhflowers.com*

**BRAND FLOWERS, INC.**
Carpinteria, California
800.549.0085 / 805.684.5531
*www.brandflowers.com*

**BRASSICA NURSERY INC.**
Nipomo, California
805.929.1550

**CALLA CO.**
Moss Landing, California
831.728.5392
*www.callaco.com*

**CAMFLOR, INC.**
Watsonville, California
888.CAM.FLOR (226.3567) / 831.726.1330
*www.camflor.com*

**EUFLORIA FLOWERS**
Nipomo, California
866.929.4683 / 805.929.4683
*www.eufloriaflowers.com*

**GALLUP & STRIBLING ORCHIDS**
Carpinteria, California
800.222.7450 / 805.684.1998
*www.gallup-stribling.com*

**GREEN VALLEY FLORAL**
Salinas, California
800.228.1255 / 831.424.7691

**JIM RIDER FLOWERS**
Watsonville, California
831.724.7285

**KENDALL FARMS**
Fallbrook, California
800.900.0848 / 760.731.0681
*www.kendall-farms.com*

**KOCH CALIFORNIA LTD.**
Nipomo, California
805.929.4153

**MAXIMUM NURSERY, INC.**
Carpinteria, California
800.GERBERA (437.2372) / 805.684.4006

**MELLANO & COMPANY**
San Luis Rey, California
800.MELLANO (635.5266) / 760.433.9550
*www.mellano.com*

**MYRIAD FLOWERS INTERNATIONAL, INC.**
Carpinteria, California
877.7MYRIAD (769.7423) / 805.684.8079
*www.myriadflowers.com*

**OBIES FLORAL, INC.**
Watsonville, California
888.313.6423 / 831.728.3636
*www.obiesfloral.com*

**OBRA VERDE GROWERS**
Valley Center, California
888.301.9029 / 760.749.2050
*www.obraverde-flowers.com*

**OCEAN BREEZE INTERNATIONAL**
Carpinteria, California
888.715.8888 / 805.684.1747
*www.oceanbreezeintl.com*

**OCEAN VIEW FLOWERS**
Lompoc, California
800.736.5608 / 805.736.5608
*www.oceanviewflowers.com*

**PAJARO VALLEY GREENHOUSES, INC.**
Watsonville, California
800.538.5922 / 831.722.2773
*www.pvflowers.com*

**PYRAMID FLOWERS, INC.**
Oxnard, California
800.338.2700 / 805.382.8070
*www.pyramidflowers.com*

**RESENDIZ BROTHERS PROTEA GROWERS LLC**
Fallbrook, California
760.731.3305
*www.resendizbrothers.com*

**THE SUN VALLEY FLORAL GROUP, INC.**
Arcata, California
800.747.0396 / 707.826.8700
*www.sunvalleyfloral.com*

**TAYAMA GREENHOUSES, INC.**
Encinitas, California
760.753.6206
*www.tayama.com*

**T. LARRY JONES, INC.**
Watsonville, California
800.424.3376 / 831.728.0320
*www.tlarryjones.com*

# credits

| | |
|---|---|
| ***Floral Designers*** | J. Keith White, AIFD |
| | Talmage McLaurin, AIFD |

## FLORISTS' REVIEW

| | |
|---|---|
| ***President*** | Frances Dudley, AAF |
| ***Publisher*** | Talmage McLaurin, AIFD |
| ***Photo Stylist*** | James Miller, AIFD |
| ***Photographer*** | Stephen Smith |
| ***Art Director*** | Ana Maben |
| ***Authors*** | Talmage McLaurin, AIFD |
| | David Coake |
| | Amy Bauer |
| ***Copy Editors*** | David Coake |
| | Kelsey Smith |

*Winning Bouquet Combinations* was produced by Florists' Review Enterprises in cooperation with the California Cut Flower Commission (CCFC).

The California Cut Flower Commission is a nonprofit public corporation formed in October 1990 by and for growers to promote California-grown cut flowers and foliages. For more information about CCFC, visit *www.ccfc.org* or call 831.462.8035.

Florists' Review Enterprises is the leading publisher of trade magazines, floral design books and other educational materials for the U.S. floral industry. Visit *www.floristsreview.com* or call 800.367.4708.

Printed in the United States by Inland Graphics, Menomonee Falls, Wisconsin

ISBN 978-0-9714860-7-2